Lilian Jackson
Braun

A Reader's Checklist
And Reference Guide

The CheckerBee Checklist™ is not authorized by Lilian Jackson Braun or any representative, agent, distributor or publisher of Lilian Jackson Braun. This publication is also not affiliated with or endorsed by any of the publications or organizations referenced within.

CheckerBee Checklist™ is a trademark of CheckerBee, Inc.

CheckerBee, Inc.
306 Industrial Park Road
Middletown, CT 06457
www.checklist.com

Copyright© 1999 CheckerBee, Inc.

All rights reserved. No part of this publication may be reproduced or transmitted in any form or by any means, electronic or mechanical, including photocopying, recording, or by any information storage or retrieval system, without the written permission of the publisher.

ISBN 1-58598-008-0

Table Of Contents

Welcome To The World Of Lilian Jackson Braun . . 5

Lilian Jackson Braun Biography 6

How To Use Your CheckerBee Checklist™ 10

Fiction 12

    The Cat Who Ate Danish Modern 12

    The Cat Who Blew the Whistle 14

    The Cat Who Came to Breakfast 16

    The Cat Who Could Read Backwards. . . 18

    The Cat Who Knew A Cardinal 20

    The Cat Who Knew Shakespeare 22

    The Cat Who Lived High 24

    The Cat Who Moved A Mountain 26

    The Cat Who Played Brahms 28

    The Cat Who Played Post Office 30

    The Cat Who Robbed A Bank 32

    The Cat Who Said Cheese 34

    The Cat Who Sang for the Birds 36

    The Cat Who Saw Red 38

Table Of Contents

The Cat Who Saw Stars 40

The Cat Who Sniffed Glue 42

The Cat Who Talked to Ghosts 44

The Cat Who Tailed A Thief 46

The Cat Who Turned On and Off 48

The Cat Who Wasn't There 50

The Cat Who Went Into the Closet 52

The Cat Who Went Underground 54

Short Story Collection 56

The Cat Who Had 14 Tales 56

Future Releases 58

Qwill, The Cats And The County. 60

Braun's Other Feline Fiction. 63

CheckerBee Checklist™ – Alphabetical 65

CheckerBee Checklist™ – Chronological 66

If You Like Lilian Jackson Braun 68

Reader's Notes 69

Welcome To The World Of Lilian Jackson Braun

*M*ystery aficionados and cat lovers, unite! Since the publication of *The Cat Who Could Read Backwards* in 1966, Lilian Jackson Braun has thrilled loyal fans with her whimsical tales of detection featuring newspaperman Jim Qwilleran and his feline friends, Koko and Yum Yum.

Now the **CheckerBee Checklist**™ brings Braun's delightful mysteries to your fingertips, covering all 22 of her novels, as well as her short story collection, *The Cat Who Had 14 Tales*. The **CheckerBee Checklist**™ includes detailed information about all of Braun's works, highlighted by summaries of each book to help you remember which ones you've read and to help you select your next reading adventure. Each title has a separate page with room for you to record your personal reading history. You can even rate the books yourself!

Other exciting features include a Lilian Jackson Braun biography, a profile of her leading characters, Qwill, Koko and Yum Yum, easy-to-use alphabetical and chronological checklists and a helpful guide to other authors you might enjoy. Happy reading!

Lilian Jackson Braun Biography

Although all of her novels so far have taken place in the upper midwestern United States, Lilian Jackson Braun is a native of New England. Most sources say she was born in Massachusetts in 1916, although Braun has never confirmed her exact date of birth. When she was still a baby, she and her family moved to Detroit.

Even as a young child, Braun showed an interest in the world of words. Her writing career began at the tender age of two when she she penned the poem "Mother Goose is up in the sky, and these are her feathers coming down in my eye." At age three, her mother taught her to write so that she could communicate with her distant grandmother. Braun attributes her success as a storyteller to her mother, who would encourage the family to tell stories of how their day went each night at the dinner table.

As a schoolgirl, Braun wrote frequently. As she mentions in an article she wrote for the "Beastly Murders" edition of *Mystery*

Lilian Jackson Braun Biography

Readers Journal, "Story-telling came to me naturally and early, and I wisely wrote about things I know: Girl Scout camp-outs, high school baseball, the eighteenth century French court."

Upon graduation from high school, Braun knew she wanted to write even more. Working with her interest in local sports, she began to sell articles to sports magazines, including *Baseball Magazine* and *The Sporting News*. Of course, in the 1930s, most readers were not yet ready to accept a female sports writer, so Braun used her only known pseudonym, Ward Jackson. She also wrote sports poems ("spoems," as she calls them), which were published in the *Detroit News*.

After a short time of this, Braun was offered a job writing ad copy for a Detroit department store. She eventually left this job and was hired by a second department store, where she was given the title of Director of Public Relations. During this time, Braun tried to write a few short stories, but never quite got them off the ground. In 1948, she took a job with the *Detroit Free Press*, writing about historical preservation, the local art scene, cooking and other topics. Eventually Braun

Lilian Jackson Braun Biography

would become the editor of the "Good Living" page, a position she would hold for nearly 30 years.

Strangely enough, Braun's life lacked the element which is common to all her mysteries – cats – until her 40th birthday. As Braun relates in an interview in *Armchair Detective* magazine, "I was forty years old when my first husband gave me a Siamese kitten for a birthday present. I really flipped over the cat. I named him Koko, after a character in Gilbert and Sullivan's *Mikado*." Sadly, the poor animal was killed in a fall from her apartment window. Some of her neighbors even raised the possibility that the cat had been pushed. The horrible ordeal would give Braun nightmares for some time after.

In an effort to deal with her grief, she wrote her first cat-oriented story, "The Sin of Madame Phloi," which was published by *Ellery Queen's Mystery Magazine*. The story was well-received and at the request of a publisher, Braun tried her hand at writing a full-length novel in 1966.

The end result was *The Cat Who Could Read Backwards*, a lighthearted "whodunit" featuring two of

Lilian Jackson Braun Biography

her signature characters, newspaper reporter Jim "Qwill" Qwilleran and his intelligent Siamese cat, Koko. The novel proved very popular and Braun followed it with two more Qwilleran-Koko novels, *The Cat Who Ate Danish Modern* (1967) and *The Cat Who Turned On and Off* (1968). Yum Yum, Koko's female companion, first appeared in *The Cat Who Ate Danish Modern* and has proven to be a capable crime-solving partner.

However, three novels about cats do not make a career, especially at a time when sex and violence were the main selling points of popular fiction. Braun took an 18-year break from her cat mysteries and continued her work with the *Detroit Free Press*. It wasn't until her retirement in the 1980s that she took up Qwill and Koko again. In 1986, *The Cat Who Saw Red* was published to rave reviews as well as an Edgar Allan Poe Award nomination from the Mystery Writers of America. Since then, Braun has penned 18 more tales featuring Qwilleran and his amazing feline friends, to the delight of millions of mystery fans and cat lovers alike.

Braun and her second husband Earl Bettinger currently live in North Carolina – along with their two Siamese cats, Koko III and Pittising.

How To Use Your CheckerBee Checklist™

IT'S A CHECKLIST *AND* A REFERENCE GUIDE!

Each book is listed with the **publication date**, the **name of the publisher** and the **page count** of the first edition. Because many titles are printed in various formats, page counts may vary.

Following the publishing information, we provide the **setting** and a **plot summary** for each title. The **CheckerBee Checklist**™ also features *The New York Times* **best-seller rankings** selected **book reviews**. Titles that have made the *The New York Times* best-seller list are noted with the highest ranking and the number of weeks on the list. The book reviews are from various respected publications, such as *Kirkus Reviews*, *Booklist* and *School Library Journal*.

The **CheckerBee Checklist**™ also provides icons for the **publishing formats** each title is available in, including *hardcover*, *paperback*, *large print* and *audio*. Only the icons applicable to that particular title will appear. Some editions may now be "out of print," which means they may be hard to find in traditional bookstores.

How To Use Your CheckerBee Checklist™

RECORD YOUR PERSONAL READING HISTORY

A complete listing of Lilian Jackson Braun's fiction titles begins on the next page, organized in alphabetical order by title. Following this is a section on her short story collection (page 56).

You can check off the "Want to Read" box to plan your future reading list. Check boxes also appear with the publishing formats, so you can keep track of which versions you own or which versions you've read or listened to. In the **Date Read** section, you can record the date you read the book. You can also rate each book on a scale from one to five stars in the **My Rating section** and put notes in the **My Comments** section.

In the **Future Releases** section on page 58, you can write in information about future books. The **Alphabetical Checklist** (page 65) and **Chronological Checklist** (page 66) can be used to record your reading history, while the **Reader's Notes** section (page 69) allows you to keep notes about your own reading adventure.

Fiction

Braun has written 22 novels in her "The Cat Who" series, including a new release scheduled for January 2000.

The Cat Who Ate Danish Modern

Want to Read

1967 • Dutton • 192 pages

Setting: "Down Below"
1960s

The *Daily Fluxion* has decided to do an interior design insert for its Sunday edition and Jim Qwilleran is dispatched to a wealthy mansion to cover the story. Just as the news feature is published, however, the home is ransacked and the owner dies under mysterious circumstances. Now it's up to Jim and his clever cat Koko to solve the crime. Jim gets a good lead when Koko takes a certain interest in the smell of some furniture in the mansion . . .

The Cat Who Ate Danish Modern

Reader's Worksheet

☐ Date Read: _____   My Rating (circle): ★ ★ ★ ★ ★

My Comments: _____

_____

_____

_____

_____

_____

_____

_____

_____

CheckerBee Note

Yum Yum, Qwilleran's second cat, is introduced in this novel. She was originally named Freya and was taken in by Qwilleran after her owner died.

The Cat Who Blew the Whistle

1995 • G.P. Putnam's Sons
240 pages

New York Times #8 — 5 Weeks On List

Setting: Moose County
1990s

Floyd Trevelyan's love for banking was only matched by his love for trains. He recently restored an old steam locomotive, turning it into a first-class party train to help boost tourism in Sawdust City.  But during the train's highly publicized debut, Floyd disappears – along with millions of dollars from the Lumbertown Credit Union, of which he is president. Adding to the mystery are a train wreck, a murder and a fatal tractor accident. Are these events somehow connected with Floyd's disappearance? Jim Qwilleran and his ever-present felines seem to think so – and they set out to find some answers.

> *"As the communicative and prescient Koko would say, 'Yow!'"*
> *–Booklist*

 Hard COVER   **PAPER** BACK   **LARGE** PRINT   Audio

The Cat Who Blew the Whistle

READER'S WORKSHEET

☐ Date Read: _____ My Rating (circle): ★ ★ ★ ★ ★

My Comments: _____

_____

_____

_____

_____

_____

_____

_____

_____

The Cat Who Came to Breakfast

1994 • G.P. Putnam's Sons
256 pages

New York Times #6
9 Weeks On List

Setting: Breakfast Island, Moose County
1990s

The tourist resort on Breakfast Island has become a risky place to take a vacation. Strange "accidents" keep striking the guests, from massive food poisoning to a deadly explosion at the marina. Natives and summer guests of Breakfast Island aren't overly fond of the tourists who invade their shores every year, but would they resort to murder to keep the outsiders from taking over? Now it's up to Jim Qwilleran and his two cat "detectives" to figure out who's behind it all.

> "Braun gives fans what they crave in this latest meandering tale about the skeptical, lovable Qwill on an island full of cats."
> *–Publishers Weekly*

The Cat Who Came to Breakfast

READER'S WORKSHEET

☐ Date Read: _____   My Rating (circle): ★ ★ ★ ★ ★

My Comments: _____

_____

_____

_____

_____

_____

_____

_____

_____

The Cat Who Could Read Backwards

1966 • Dutton • 250 pages approx.

Setting: "Down Below"
1960s

Jim Qwilleran's career as a hard-nosed reporter has been a bit slow, so when he's offered a job as a feature writer for the *Daily Fluxion*, he accepts – even though his new beat is the art community. Qwill soon meets George Bonifield Mountclemens III, the paper's acid-penned art critic, who offers him a small apartment in return for watching his Siamese cat, Koko.

But Qwill is soon on the crime beat when the only gallery Mountclemens has ever praised is vandalized and its owner stabbed to death. When Mountclemens also turns up murdered, Qwill and Koko start putting pieces together to find the killer.

"Delight from beginning to end."
–Los Angeles Times

The Cat Who Could Read Backwards

Reader's Worksheet

☐ Date Read: _____ My Rating (circle): ★ ★ ★ ★ ★

My Comments: _____

CheckerBee Note

This book, which was originally published in paperback, was issued in hardcover for the first time by Putnam in 1997.

The Cat Who Knew A Cardinal

1991 • G.P. Putnam's Sons
240 pages

New York Times #11 — 3 Weeks On List

Setting: Pickax City
1990s

When the curtain goes down on the final night of the local theater's production of *Henry VIII*, director Hilary VanBrook doesn't know it's also the closing chapter of his own life. When he's found murdered that night, no one in town is really shocked – VanBrook was well-known for his harsh, condescending ways. What's shocking is that his body lies in the apple orchard behind Jim Qwilleran's home, where the play's cast has just celebrated. Is one of the local actors playing the role of murderer? It's up to Qwill – with a little help from Koko and Yum Yum – to go on the prowl in search of answers.

"Some of the most witty original fare in the genre."
–New York Daily News

The Cat Who Knew A Cardinal

Reader's Worksheet

☐ Date Read: _____   My Rating (circle): ★ ★ ★ ★ ★

My Comments: _____

_____

_____

_____

_____

_____

_____

_____

_____

The Cat Who Knew Shakespeare

1988 • Jove • 202 pages

Setting: Pickax City
1980s

As a former reporter, Jim Qwilleran takes a special interest in his town's newspaper, the *Pickax Picayune*. He even shows Junior Goodwinter, the paper's young managing editor, the ropes of the newspaper biz, so it's only natural for him to get involved when Junior's father, the *Picayune*'s publisher, is killed in an accident. Junior wants the business to stay in the family, but his mother is anxious to sell it, along with many of the family's heirlooms. This catches Qwill's interest, which is deepened when the *Picayune* building catches fire. Now Qwill has a major mystery on his hands – and the solution may lie in Koko's sudden interest in Shakespearean plays . . .

> "A comfortable, quaint diversion . . ."
> *–Library Journal*

The Cat Who Knew Shakespeare

Reader's Worksheet

☐ Date Read: _____   My Rating (circle): ★ ★ ★ ★ ★

My Comments: _____

_____

_____

_____

_____

_____

_____

_____

_____

The Cat Who Lived High

1990 • G.P. Putnam's Sons • 240 pages

Want to Read

Setting: "Down Below"
1990s

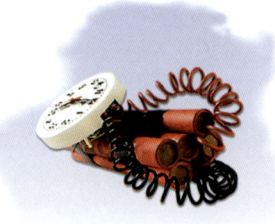

When an old acquaintance of Jim Qwilleran's tells him that there will be an attempt to tear down the Casablanca, a beautiful but old apartment building, Qwill offers to help out with capital from the Klingenschoen Fund. Jim and his two cats move into the penthouse temporarily. But soon after their arrival, Qwill makes an unsettling discovery – the previous tenant, a pretentious art dealer, was murdered in that very apartment. It doesn't take Qwill and the cats long to figure out that the murder and the building's impending destruction may be related.

". . . a delight that will enchant long-time followers of the irresistible trio as well as first-time readers."
–School Library Journal

The Cat Who Lived High

Reader's Worksheet

☐ Date Read: _____ My Rating (circle): ★ ★ ★ ★ ★

My Comments: _____

_____

_____

_____

_____

_____

_____

_____

_____

_____

The Cat Who Moved A Mountain

☐ Want to Read

1992 • G.P. Putnam's Sons
240 pages

New York Times #9 — 5 Weeks On List

Setting: Spudsboro
1990s

Needing a change of scenery, Jim Qwilleran and his cats head to Big Potato Mountain for a summer vacation. But as luck would have it, they arrive in the midst of chaos. A corporation wants  to develop the area for tourism, an environmental group wants to keep the area pristine and the local farmers want both sides out of the picture. Qwill learns that the house he's rented belonged to J.J. Hawkinfield, a real estate mogul who supported development – and turned up murdered. But did the wrong man go to jail for the crime? It's up to Qwill and the cats to uncover the truth.

> " . . . a lively, witty tale bolstered by sharply etched characters."
> *–Publishers Weekly*

☐ **Hard** COVER   ☐ **PAPER** BACK   ☐ **LARGE** PRINT   ☐ Audio

26   Fiction

The Cat Who Moved A Mountain

Reader's Worksheet

☐ Date Read: _____   My Rating (circle): ⭐ ⭐ ⭐ ⭐ ⭐

My Comments: _____

_____

_____

_____

_____

_____

_____

_____

_____

_____

Fiction

The Cat Who Played Brahms

1987 • G.P. Putnam's Sons • 192 pages

Setting: Mooseville
1980s

After so many years of working for the *Daily Fluxion*, Jim Qwilleran is fed up. He decides to take a few weeks off and spend some time in rural Moose County, where his beloved Aunt Fanny Klingenschoen has a lakeside house.  But something's not quite right about the place. The area's residents are a close-mouthed, conspiratorial lot who won't tell him anything when Aunt Fanny turns up dead. But Qwill has the aid of his beloved cats to help him turn up clues to this troublesome mystery.

The Cat Who Played Brahms

Reader's Worksheet

☐ Date Read: _____   My Rating (circle): ⭐ ⭐ ⭐ ⭐ ⭐

My Comments: _____

_____

_____

_____

_____

_____

_____

_____

_____

The Cat Who Played Post Office

1987 • G.P. Putnam's Sons • 186 pages

Setting: Moose County
Late 1980s

Having received a hefty inheritance upon his Aunt Fanny's untimely death, Jim Qwilleran tries to adjust to the life of a rich country gentleman at Klingenschoen Mansion. But his new home holds a bit of a secret. Years before, a young housemaid had vanished under mysterious circumstances. And when a murder is committed, it looks as if someone wants to be sure that secret remains hidden. What promised to be a life of carefree ease turns into a whirlwind mystery as Qwill enlists his faithful cats to help him put the pieces together.

The Cat Who Played Post Office

Reader's Worksheet

☐ Date Read: _____ My Rating (circle): ⭐ ⭐ ⭐ ⭐ ⭐

My Comments: _____

The Cat Who Robbed A Bank

☐ Want to Read

To Be Released January 2000
G.P. Putnam's Sons

Reader's Summary: _____

_____

_____

_____

_____

_____

_____

Coming Soon!

_____

_____

_____

_____

Look for this upcoming new title by
Lilian Jackson Braun in January 2000!

The Cat Who Robbed A Bank

Reader's Worksheet

☐ Date Read: _____ My Rating (circle): ★ ★ ★ ★ ★

My Comments: _____

The Cat Who Said Cheese

1996 • G.P. Putnam's Sons
246 pages

New York Times #5 — 6 Weeks On List

Setting: Pickax City
1990s

Residents of Pickax City are gearing up for their first annual Great Food Explo, an event highlighting local restaurants, bakeries and wine and cheese shops. But the Explo isn't the only talk of the town – there also is the mysterious woman dressed all in black who's checked into the New Pickax Hotel. A short time later, a bomb destroys the hotel and the mysterious woman disappears as suddenly as she arrived. Now it's up to Jim Qwilleran, with precious few clues, to solve the case – aided by his cats and their recent interest in cheese . . .

> "An ingenious plot, colorful characters, and delightful humor . . ."
> *–Booklist*

The Cat Who Said Cheese

READER'S WORKSHEET

☐ Date Read: _____ My Rating (circle): ★ ★ ★ ★ ★

My Comments: _____

The Cat Who Sang for the Birds

1998 • G.P. Putnam's Sons
248 pages

New York Times #5 — 6 Weeks On List

Setting: Pickax City
1990s

Pickax's new art gallery is a welcome addition to the town. But many residents are sick of looking at a particularly sorry old home across the street from the gallery. When the woman who lives there dies in a mysterious fire, Jim Qwilleran discovers that she had just sold her huge farm to a dummy corporation. Meanwhile, the art gallery is broken into, and Qwill and his cats  must discover just who bought the old property, as well as how these events are connected.

"A light, entertaining whodunit that offers the added appeal of cats and their often mysterious ways."
–*School Library Journal*

36   Fiction

The Cat Who Sang for the Birds

READER'S WORKSHEET

☐ Date Read: _____   My Rating (circle): ★ ★ ★ ★ ★

My Comments: _____

_____

_____

_____

_____

_____

_____

_____

_____

_____

_____

The Cat Who Saw Red

1986 • Jove • 192 pages approx.

Setting: Moose County
1980s

Jim Qwilleran has become the new food and wine writer for the *Daily Fluxion*. His first story is on the Maus Haus, a boarding house of sorts owned by an extraordinary cook. Much to Qwill's surprise, one of the tenants is Joy Wheatley, his first love who deserted him. The two spend an evening catching up, and Qwill learns that Joy is unhappily married and low on cash. He lends her money, only to wake up the next morning to learn she has disappeared. Was it Joy's scream he heard in the middle of the night? Was Joy in that car he saw driving away at 3 o'clock in the morning? Qwill suspects danger and, with the help of his cats, is determined to find the truth.

". . . a delightful tale."
–*Publishers Weekly*

Fiction

The Cat Who Saw Red

READER'S WORKSHEET

☐ Date Read: _____   My Rating (circle): ★ ★ ★ ★ ★

My Comments: _____

Fiction

The Cat Who Saw Stars

1999 • G.P. Putnam's Sons
227 pages

Setting: Moose County
1990s

Jim Qwilleran and his crime-solving cats are on their way to Mooseville for a month's vacation at the beach when they learn that a lone hiker has disappeared there. Rumors abound around

town that the hiker has been abducted by aliens, because the area has a long history of unusual disappearances alleged to be at the hands of aliens, or "Visitors," as the locals call them. Ever the skeptic, Qwill doesn't buy it – until Koko becomes newly fascinated with the stars in the night sky.

"Koko and Yum Yum star in their 21st novel here,
and . . . they're still the cat's meow."
–*Publishers Weekly*

Fiction

The Cat Who Saw Stars

Reader's Worksheet

☐ Date Read: _____   My Rating (circle): ★ ★ ★ ★ ★

My Comments: _____

The Cat Who Sniffed Glue

1988 • G.P. Putnam's Sons • 207 pages

Setting: Pickax City
1980s

Normally, Pickax City is a quiet rural setting, free from the problems of the big city. But lately things have been different. Vandalism and destruction of property are becoming a problem, and when Harley and Belle Fitch, a notable local couple, are found shot to death, it seems Pickax will never be the same. The local law thinks low-class ruffians from the next town over are to blame. But when Koko and Yum Yum develop a strange fondness for glue, Jim Qwilleran suspects that it's not that simple.

The Cat Who Sniffed Glue

Reader's Worksheet

☐ Date Read: _____   My Rating (circle): ★ ★ ★ ★ ★

My Comments: _____

_____

_____

_____

_____

_____

_____

_____

_____

The Cat Who Talked to Ghosts

1990 • G.P. Putnam's Sons
224 pages

New York Times #10 — 5 Weeks On List

Setting: Pickax City
1990s

Iris Cobb is literally scared to death one October evening. Mrs. Cobb, the live-in manager of the Goodwinter Farmhouse Museum, calls her good friend Jim Qwilleran in a panic on the night of her death, complaining about odd rattling and moaning in the walls of the old building. But by the time Qwill arrives to check on Mrs. Cobb, she is already dead. Qwill senses a mystery, so he packs up Koko and Yum Yum and settles into the Goodwinter Farmhouse Museum to solve the case.

> "The mix of crime and cats is catnip to readers who like both."
> *–Chicago Sun-Times*

The Cat Who Talked to Ghosts

Reader's Worksheet

☐ Date Read: _____ My Rating (circle): ★ ★ ★ ★ ★

My Comments: _____

_____

_____

_____

_____

_____

_____

_____

_____

_____

The Cat Who Tailed A Thief

1997 • G.P. Putnam's Sons
256 pages

New York Times #9 — 5 Weeks On List

Setting: Pickax City
1990s

A lot of action has come to Pickax lately. Minor thefts have been occurring throughout the city, the new banker Willard Carmichael and his wife Danielle have just moved to town and Carter Lee James, Danielle's cousin, has arrived to renovate historic "Gingerbread Alley." Are all these events coincidental? Jim Qwilleran doesn't think so, and becomes convinced of it when a decent local boy is accused of the thefts and some mysterious deaths occur. And the recent actions of his cats Koko and Yum Yum are making Jim even more suspicious . . .

> ". . . an accomplished mystery that is as smooth as the seasonal snowfall."
> –*Publishers Weekly*

46   Fiction

The Cat Who Tailed A Thief

Reader's Worksheet

☐ Date Read: _____ My Rating (circle): ⭐ ⭐ ⭐ ⭐ ⭐

My Comments: _____

The Cat Who Turned On and Off

1968 • Dutton • 186 pages

Setting: Junktown
1960s

Jim Qwilleran, reporter for the *Daily Fluxion,* hopes to do a feature story on the seedy side of Junktown, but his editor instead assigns him to a piece on the antiques for which Junktown is famous.

Qwill is slightly disappointed, but finds that the story is more exciting than he had anticipated. While researching an auction of a recently deceased dealer's inventory, he senses that the death was no accident. With the capable help of Koko and Yum Yum, Qwill must assemble the pieces of this puzzle before time runs out.

The Cat Who Turned On and Off

Reader's Worksheet

☐ Date Read: _____ My Rating (circle): ★ ★ ★ ★ ★

My Comments: _____

_____

_____

_____

_____

_____

_____

_____

_____

_____

The Cat Who Wasn't There

1992 • G.P. Putnam's Sons
238 pages

Setting: Scotland and Pickax City
1990s

Polly Duncan, the object of Jim Qwilleran's affection, is being stalked. To get her out of harm's way, Qwill plans a trip to the Scottish Highlands with a group of Pickax City residents.

Things run smoothly until the tour guide dies, the tour bus driver vanishes and a suitcase full of jewelry disappears. Meanwhile, across the ocean, Koko and Yum Yum sense something bad is going on. And when Qwill comes home, they'll be the ones to help him crack this case.

> "Braun's descriptions of Scottish lore and the complications of Qwill's love life will enchant fans."
> *–Publishers Weekly*

The Cat Who Wasn't There

READER'S WORKSHEET

☐ Date Read: _____ My Rating (circle): ★ ★ ★ ★ ★

My Comments: _____

_____

_____

_____

_____

_____

_____

_____

_____

_____

_____

The Cat Who Went Into the Closet

1993 • G.P. Putnam's Sons
235 pages

New York Times #15 — 1 Week On List

Setting: Pickax City
1990s

Jim Qwilleran has decided to rent the Gage mansion from his friend Junior Goodwinter for the winter season. The giant home once belonged to Junior's grandmother Euphonia Gage, who now lives a happy life in Florida – at least until she commits suicide. Qwill is suspicious – especially when a local farmer is murdered soon after. Are the two incidents related? And is there any significance to the items Koko keeps bringing out of the many over-stuffed closets in the mansion? Qwill wants to find out, and enlists his cats to help.

> ". . . sure to be enjoyed by the author's devoted following."
> *–Kirkus Reviews*

Fiction

The Cat Who Went Into the Closet

READER'S WORKSHEET

☐ Date Read: _____ My Rating (circle): ★ ★ ★ ★ ★

My Comments: _____

_____

_____

_____

_____

_____

_____

_____

_____

_____

The Cat Who Went Underground

1988 • G.P. Putnam's Sons • 224 pages

☐ Want to Read

Setting: Moose County
1980s

Normally, Jim Qwilleran is the one solving the crimes – now, he's the one being questioned for murder. It all begins when he heads to his lakefront cabin for three months of summer relaxation. He has plans to build an addition onto the cabin, but mysteriously, the carpenters he hires keep disappearing. When one of them is found dead beneath Qwill's house, questions are asked. Now it's up to the cats alone to clear his name.

"Breezy and amusing. . ."
–Publishers Weekly

☐ **Hard** COVER   ☐ **PAPER** BACK   ☐ **LARGE** PRINT

54   Fiction

The Cat Who Went Underground

Reader's Worksheet

- [ ] Date Read: _____   My Rating (circle): ★ ★ ★ ★ ★

My Comments: _____

Short Story Collection

This is the only short story anthology that is dedicated to the work of Lilian Jackson Braun.

The Cat Who Had 14 Tales

1988 • Jove • 184 pages

This collection of 14 short stories includes "A Cat Named Conscience," "A Cat Too Small for His Whiskers," "The Dark One," "East Side Story," "The Fluppie Phenomenon," "The Hero of Drummond Street," "The Mad Museum Mouser," "Phut Phat Concentrates," "The Sin of Madame Phloi," "Stanley and Spook," "SuSu and the 8:30 Ghost," "Tipsy and the Board of Health," "Tragedy on New Year's Eve" and "Weekend of the Big Puddle."

The Cat Who Had 14 Tales

READER'S WORKSHEET

☐ Date Read: _____   My Rating (circle): ★ ★ ★ ★ ★

My Comments: _____

_____

_____

_____

_____

_____

_____

_____

_____

CHECKERBEE NOTE

This collection features a combination of short stories previously published in 1960s-era mystery magazines and more recent, never-before-published stories.

Future Release

This page can be used to write in information about a future Lilian Jackson Braun release.

Title:

☐ Want to Read

Publication Date:
Name Of Publisher:
Page Count:

Setting:

Reader's Summary: _____

_____

_____

Future Release

_____

_____

_____

_____

☐ Date Read: _____ My Rating (circle): ★ ★ ★ ★ ★

My Comments: _____

_____

_____

_____

Future Release

This page can be used to write in information about a future Lilian Jackson Braun release.

Title:

☐ Want to Read

Publication Date:
Name Of Publisher:
Page Count:

Setting:

Reader's Summary:

_____

_____

_____

_____

_____

Future Release

☐ Date Read: _____ My Rating (circle): ★ ★ ★ ★ ★

My Comments: _____

_____

_____

_____

Qwill, The Cats And The County

James Mackintosh Qwilleran, Lilian Jackson Braun's human detective, is the quintessential lovable curmudgeon. His most significant trait is his famous mustache – a wide, bushy, salt-and-pepper creation that tingles like a cat's whisker when he's found a clue.

A divorced, middle-aged, recovering alcoholic, Qwill (as everyone calls him) says that he has no desire to remarry, and is perfectly content as a bachelor. He has sad eyes that perhaps carry melancholy memories of the past. However, he's always gentlemanly and courteous, generous and friendly, and well-liked by everyone who knows him.

He worked as a correspondent with many papers throughout the country before deciding to join the staff of the *Daily Fluxion* in Down Below. He later starts up his own newspaper, the *Moose County Something*, for which he writes a bi-weekly column called "Straight from the Qwill Pen."

Qwill, The Cats And The County

When he inherits a vast fortune after the death of his mother's dearest friend, Qwill could have become selfish and extravagant. Instead he puts the money to good use in the form of the Klingenshoen Foundation, a fund developed to better the society of Moose County, a pleasantly rural backwater where Qwill makes his home.

But Qwill would be nothing without his cats. In *The Cat Who Read Backwards,* Qwill ends up owning (or being owned by, depending on your cat experience) a moody and demanding male Siamese cat named K'ao Ko Kung (Koko for short). In the next book, *The Cat Who Ate Danish Modern,* Qwill adopts Yum Yum, a female Siamese cat, as a companion for the lonely Koko.

Qwill is an intelligent, perceptive man, but his cats – especially Koko – have an almost supernatural ability to sniff out clues that he has somehow missed. Koko and Yum Yum have the personalities of a crime-fighting couple, with Koko providing the solutions and Yum Yum close behind to help out.

Qwill, The Cats And The County

The feline sleuths, however, are not without their unpleasant sides. Both of them are finicky to the point of obsession, and insist on fresh food – nothing out of a can, please! They live in their own apartment inside Qwill's home, and even have their own television and private bath! The cats are also profoundly possessive of their human; neither of them like any of Qwill's lady friends, and they act agitated if they sense he's been around another cat.

Perhaps the most distinctive feature of "The Cat Who . . ." books is their sense of setting. Moose County is described as "400 miles north of everywhere." It is never specifically disclosed just where Moose County is, or to which city "Down Below" refers. Most readers place the stories somewhere in Michigan, Wisconsin or Minnesota, but no one will ever really be sure. In Moose County, Braun has created a beautiful example of rural small-town life, where the height of local gatherings is the annual spelling bee and the number one vice is idle gossip. In short, a perfect setting for a cozy mystery.

Braun's Other Feline Fiction

*L*ilian Jackson Braun found fame with "The Cat Who . . ." books, but her career was launched when her short stories about cats were published in *Ellery Queen's Mystery Magazine*, a  publication that showcases mystery authors. Despite her current success, Braun continues to write short works of fiction for collections.

The Mystery Writers of America included one of Braun's short stories in 1989's *Beastly Tales: The Mystery Writers of America Anthology* edited by Sara Paretsky. The following year, Braun was included in an anthology of female crime authors entitled *Sisters in Crime 3,* edited by Marilyn Wallace.

Braun's stories were included in a trio of books released in the early 1990s called *Mystery Cats*, *More Mystery Cats* and *Mystery Cats III*. Each book contains over a dozen stories by mystery writers who favor felines.

Her work can also be found in 1994's *Mysterious Cat Stories*, which was edited by John Richard

Braun's Other Feline Fiction

Stephens and Kim Smith and features a collection of more than 20 spooky stories about felines. An anthology that included stories that previously appeared in *Ellery Queen's Mystery Magazine* and *Alfred Hitchcock Mystery Magazine* was published in 1996 under the name *Mysterious Menagerie*. This collection includes Braun's "Stanley and Spook."

Braun wrote the foreword in a 1997 primer for cat owners entitled *Cats for Dummies*™ co-authored by Gina Spadafori and Paul Pion. Former ASPCA President Roger Caras included Braun's story "Phut Phat Concentrates" in his 1997 book *The New Roger Caras Treasury of Great Cat Stories: A Collection of Tales That Celebrates the Mystique and Charm of Cats*.

For her most recent contribution, Braun received top billing on the cover of 1998's *Midnight Louie's Pet Detectives*, edited by Carole Nelson Douglas.

Koko and Yum Yum aren't Braun's only creations. To learn more about her other felines, visit your favorite library or bookseller to find the anthologies mentioned here.

CheckerBee Checklist™
Alphabetical

This alphabetical checklist of Lilian Jackson Braun's published works is a great way to keep track of which books you have read or which books you want to read.

Fiction
- ❏ The Cat Who Ate Danish Modern
- ❏ The Cat Who Blew the Whistle
- ❏ The Cat Who Came to Breakfast
- ❏ The Cat Who Could Read Backwards
- ❏ The Cat Who Knew A Cardinal
- ❏ The Cat Who Knew Shakespeare
- ❏ The Cat Who Lived High
- ❏ The Cat Who Moved A Mountain
- ❏ The Cat Who Played Brahms
- ❏ The Cat Who Played Post Office
- ❏ The Cat Who Robbed A Bank
- ❏ The Cat Who Said Cheese
- ❏ The Cat Who Sang for the Birds
- ❏ The Cat Who Saw Red
- ❏ The Cat Who Saw Stars
- ❏ The Cat Who Sniffed Glue
- ❏ The Cat Who Talked to Ghosts
- ❏ The Cat Who Tailed A Thief
- ❏ The Cat Who Turned On and Off
- ❏ The Cat Who Wasn't There
- ❏ The Cat Who Went Into the Closet
- ❏ The Cat Who Went Underground

Short Story Collection
- ❏ The Cat Who Had 14 Tales

CheckerBee Checklist™
Chronological

This chronological checklist includes all of Lilian Jackson Braun's published works in order of the publication dates, from her earliest to her most recent.

Fiction Chronology

- ❏ The Cat Who Could Read Backwards *1966*
- ❏ The Cat Who Ate Danish Modern *1967*
- ❏ The Cat Who Turned On and Off *1968*
- ❏ The Cat Who Saw Red . . . . *August 1986*
- ❏ The Cat Who Played Brahms . . . . *June 1987*
- ❏ The Cat Who Played Post Office . . *December 1987*
- ❏ The Cat Who Knew Shakespeare . . . . . . *June 1988*
- ❏ The Cat Who Sniffed Glue . . . . . . *September 1988*
- ❏ The Cat Who Went Underground . . . *March 1989*
- ❏ The Cat Who Talked to Ghosts . . . . *January 1990*

Fiction Chronology, cont.

- ❏ The Cat Who Lived High . . . . *August 1990*

- ❏ The Cat Who Knew A Cardinal . . . . . . *May 1991*

- ❏ The Cat Who Moved A Mountain . *February 1992*

- ❏ The Cat Who Wasn't There. . . . . . *September 1992*

- ❏ The Cat Who Went Into the Closet . . . *May 1993*

- ❏ The Cat Who Came to Breakfast . . *February 1994*

- ❏ The Cat Who Blew the Whistle . . . *February 1995*

- ❏ The Cat Who Said Cheese . . . . *February 1996*

- ❏ The Cat Who Tailed A Thief . . . . . *February 1997*

- ❏ The Cat Who Sang for the Birds . . . *January 1998*

- ❏ The Cat Who Saw Stars . . . . *January 1999*

- ❏ The Cat Who Robbed A Bank . . . . . *January 2000*

Short Story Collection Chronology

- ❏ The Cat Who Had 14 Tales . . . . *March 1988*

If You Like Lilian Jackson Braun . . .

Here are some other authors you might enjoy!

LYDIA ADAMSON

Alice Nestleton works as a catsitter while in between acting jobs. But with the help of her furry friends, she's an unstoppable sleuth. Adamson's works include *A Cat on Jingle Bell Rock* and *A Cat on a Beach Blanket*.

GARRISON ALLEN

Bookstore owner Penelope Warren and her feline companion, Big Mike, help keep Empty Creek, Arizona crime-free as they take on a series of murderers and kidnappers. Try *Stable Cat, Movie Cat* or *Baseball Cat*.

MARIAN BABSON

You'll be glued to the edge of your seat as you read Marian Babson's tales of crime and suspense. *Whiskers and Smoke* and *Nine Lives to Murder* are some of her titles.

CAROLE NELSON DOUGLAS

Carole Nelson Douglas is the creative force behind cat detective Midnight Louie and his owner, public relations guru Temple Barr. Try *Catnap* or *Cat in a Flamingo Fedora*.

My Favorite Bookstores/Libraries

My Favorite Books

Great Reading Web Sites

www.checklist.com

My Reading List

Books Borrowed/Books Loaned

NOTES

Check out our other great titles!

AUTHORS

- V.C. Andrews
  ISBN 1-58598-006-4
- Barbara Taylor Bradford
  ISBN 1-58598-007-2
- Lilian Jackson Braun
  ISBN 1-58598-008-0
- Orson Scott Card
  ISBN 1-58598-009-9
- Agatha Christie
  ISBN 1-58598-010-2
- Tom Clancy
  ISBN 1-58598-011-0
- Mary Higgins Clark
  ISBN 1-58598-012-9
- Robin Cook
  ISBN 1-58598-013-7
- Patricia Cornwell
  ISBN 1-58598-014-5
- Michael Crichton
  ISBN 1-58598-015-3
- Nelson DeMille
  ISBN 1-58598-016-1
- Ken Follett
  ISBN 1-58598-017-X
- Dick Francis
  ISBN 1-58598-018-8
- Sue Grafton
  ISBN 1-58598-019-6
- John Grisham
  ISBN 1-58598-020-X
- Tony Hillerman
  ISBN 1-58598-021-8
- P.D. James
  ISBN 1-58598-022-6
- Robert Jordan
  ISBN 1-58598-023-4
- Stephen King
  ISBN 1-58598-024-2
- Dean Koontz
  ISBN 1-58598-025-0
- Elmore Leonard
  ISBN 1-58598-026-9
- Robert Ludlum
  ISBN 1-58598-027-7
- Larry McMurtry
  ISBN 1-58598-028-5
- James Michener
  ISBN 1-58598-029-3
- Toni Morrison
  ISBN 1-58598-030-7
- James Patterson
  ISBN 1-58598-031-5
- Anne Rice
  ISBN 1-58598-032-3
- Nora Roberts
  ISBN 1-58598-033-1
- Sidney Sheldon
  ISBN 1-58598-034-X
- Danielle Steel
  ISBN 1-58598-035-8

GENRES

- Children's Picture Books
  ISBN 1-58598-000-5
- Detective Mysteries
  ISBN 1-58598-001-3
- Historical Romance
  ISBN 1-58598-002-1
- Legal Thrillers
  ISBN 1-58598-003-X
- Science Fiction
  ISBN 1-58598-004-8
- Young Adult Fiction
  ISBN 1-58598-005-6

Send your suggestions for future editions to:
suggestions@checklist.com